"GET RICH GUIDE"

C. Edward Royce @2010.

WISDOM WORDS

"IN THE BEGINNING"

FORWARDS

Dear Readers:

Actually I hadn't intended to write this now?
Or indeed anything even remotely like it''
Yet 'being' troubled both in heart.

And in spirit,.

For the -greatest writer- of all!.
(No not myself).

But the "Holy Spirit" has nudged me into
writing this account.

So at His -urging' I pen (Or write) again this
new book as He would have me do it.

And speaking "frankly" the more I write
this.

Then all the more I can understand the
meaning?,.

Meaning?.

"What Meaning"?.

Of the urgent or 'pressing' need for this
book.

As its clear of the vital need for a:

"Bible based book on Finance".

Yes I realize thats a tall order!.

(A very great one actually?).

But the need exists, And the facts are plain.

And Surely:

Yet why now?.

Well a quick glance at the morning paper.

Or just listening in on the car radio!.

Yes even for just a 'few' moments reveals:

Terrible things!.

Hardship and Suffering!.

For the facts are plain.

And the "truth" is there for all to see,And to see clearly at that!.

So why not -face- the truth?.

'Joblessness and Want!.

Or:

Homelessness and Hunger!.

"Truly"

"And these conditions are real".

Yes thats right!.

Poverty and Hopelessness.

And in the "Richest Nation" on Earth!.

That being the case we think!.

And again we pray:

"What can we do"!.

And isn't there an answer somewhere?.

Yes surely!.

And some of the answers that may be of benefIt.

To You;

And to Me and to all the rest of Us!.

May be right here in the following pages.

And why not?.

Indeed for man was -not- created to be:

'Needy and Poor'.

Or to suffer in want!.

Yes there is Hope!,.

For if we look hard enough.

And search long enough.

An answer can usually be found?.

"As is usually the case in life".

With the need being evident.

Still:

We know that times are tough.

And that money -is- short.

And thats a certainty given the terrible economic times we live in?.

While "NO" book (this one included) has all the answers.

Yet the story it tells!.

And the principals it contains can help you!.

And guide you!.

Perhaps even giving you a running start to rebuild a prosperous you.

And better yet!.

Possibly even help you form a game plan for the future?.

Thats right.

"Your Future"!.

That being the case I respectfully write these pages as 'The Spirit' inspires me to provide hope!.

(Blessed be His name!).

Yet while written for Christians in mind.

The principals and guidelines involved may prove of help to all if used properly?.

In Addition:

There is a 'Resource' section at the end to provide some help if you feel the need?.

Yes I know -its- tough!.

But please don't get discouraged.

For we should 'always' remember!.

That a great and "Mighty God" wants to help.

And whats better He wrote a book to help us in our need.

5

That book is called the Bible!.

And it has principals for living!.

"Also for creating wealth".

Plus restoring your Finances!.

And many of those 'amazing' principals.

"Bible Principals"!

Are outlined in this book were about to read.

After all didn't Jesus Himself rely on the principals and teachings of the Bible!.

So why shouldn't we ?.

That being the case :Dear Reader!.

Lets examine the 1st principal in this book.

"There is always hope".

And secondly:

"Always trust in God".

And finally if you haven't received Jesus yet then please do so and your blessings will unfold!.

That being said and done.

Lets look ahead both to the principals!.

(And the persons outlined in this book).

For the studies enclosed will be of much use to you in your walk in life.

For the goal is always worthy of the journey

And since Life itself is a Journey!.

Then lets take the first step and go forwards shall we!.

C. Edward Royce,.

CHAPTERS

CHAPTER .1

"BIBLE PRINCIPALS OF FINANCE"

WISDOM WORDS

'FOR LACK OF KNOWLEDGE MY PEOPLE'
"ARE DESTROYED"

I cant pay the rent!.

OR:

"I'm back on the car payment".

The kids need 'school stuff'?.

Sounds familiar right!.

But my -favorite- is.

Oh! I'm broke can you lend me a twenty?.

Yes and I'm sure in your town that you've heard all of the above,.

And some to be sure that are 'worse'!.

(Perhaps even appalling at times).

Granted that its all sad and even sorry too.

After all we (in America) are in the richest and most prosperous nation on Earth!,.

Yet again the words:

Ring out;

"I'm broke"?.

And how?.

For is everybody broke and poor also'.

"Yes dear readers a core essential point is being discussed here".

OR:

Should we look at this another way.

Could it be that?.

Perhaps !.

Or -just- maybe the real problem is that we are simply not using our money wisely.

And we definitely should look at balance here.

Lets say then :

That one person may earn a hundred thousand a year?.

(A -nice-sum in this economy).

Whereas someone else may earn perhaps thirty thousand a year?.

And yet another just 'Fifteen or Twelve thousand ' a year?.

So lets then look at the heart of the matter a little bit closer!.

And truly pay scales and salaries will vary widely.

(Or maybe some would say wildly)!.

Yet looked at closely the fry-cook at Mc Donalds will make more money than you do in ten years!.

Still how is that possible?.

Well its easy if you look at the heart of the matter.

OR:

If the 'fry-cook- regularly saves and invests his money?.

"And -YOU- don't'?,.

True it "sounds" incredible.

And -even- impossible!.

Until you learn to understand the "strength" and power of numbers?.

And -compound- interest!.

OR:

Expressed simply the person who saves money.

And who learns to re-invest it.

Will always make more than the person who "doesn't" save or invest money!.

And yes it really is 'THAT' simple.

However:

There is a very strict or cardinal difference involved?.

(Actually a very great one!).

For "God" Himself advises:

"My people are destroyed for lack of knowledge"!.

And that being true is one thing we are going to try and correct with this book,.

A good case in point being:

The difference between making money!.

And -earning- money?.

Granted that many out there are now shaking their heads.

Yes I know, I know.

Its difficult!.

But again its only as -difficult- as you yourself make it?.

(The difference is plain but 'important')!.

Expressed simply:

The difference being that making money is the salary.

Or if you prefer the daily wage that you are getting paid for getting up each morning and dragging yourself!.

(Or herself!).

Off to work each and every morning!.

Being basically the cash compensation your job or company pays in return for your time and labors.

Now the other side or:

Earning money is considerably different!.

(And -very- much so!).

Again and expressed simply:

Earning money is the cash compensation you earn -without- going to work!.

(See 'very' different).

Now earned funds (or cash) can come from many sources?.

Say the interest your bank pays you for your interest bearing bonds, Or notes or bank CDs etc etc!.

Oh to be sure there are some gray areas.

Like a pension fund!.

Or say an "inheritance"!. Or insurance?.

As in a sense you are being paid now mainly in return for past work.

Or efforts to benefit an employer or a company etc.

Though there can be many forms this stated is the basic idea between making and earning money!.

Yet it must be said and at once that:

There is a 3rd way to make money.

And even to realize "a profit"?.

That way is to 'save' money.

For it isn't what you make, But what you save that counts!.

But we will go into detail on that a bit later on in this book.

Then again the Bible itself also advises us on these issues?.

Still the real (and sorry) truth is that Americans from 'all' income groups tend to spend far more than they make!.

And whats far worse is that many people.

(Some well meaning!).

Go and 'borrow' even more money to fund and pay for their lifestyles?.

Once again we -see- and are instructed in the difficulty if we look at the Bible.

After all didn't no less a teacher than John the Baptist instruct us to:

"Be satisfied with our wages"?.

Now the other side of the coin is also very well true as we see that;

Borrowing money is one of the -worst- things you can do!.

Yes, Yes I know that strikes a wrong cord with many out there.

But still:

How can you make,.

Or earn money?.

If you are constantly borrowing,Preferring to remain eternally in debt?.

For God Himself is 'specific' in this matter.

He teaches us in "Psalms and Proverbs";

"Lend but do not Borrow"!.

Another teaching very much to the point here also is :

"The Debtor (you) is the Slave to the Lender".

(IE: the Bank!).

All right still not convinced?.

Jesus Himself can be seen in making a reference to debt when He said:

The seed (your cash) is sown into rocks (or just wasted)!,.

And Jesus is without doubt the smartest man who ever lived.

Looking back it seems that John the Baptist also taught us that:

"Don't live outside your means".

OR:

"Do not spend more money than you make"

So it would appear that:

You -cant- make money if you are always in debt, Or always borrowing?.

And: Dear Reader.

It would appear that Jesus tends to advise us somewhat similarly!.

For His parable of the seed in the rock may also mean that;

"Don't waste your money"!.

And!.

Or throw it away into -unprofitable- areas that do -not- offer a return?.

Its starting to make sense now isn't it.

And money and 'financial' issues are a hard area to advise people in.

For its easy to tell people!.

Do not drink.

OR:

Do not use drugs!.

But people are very defensive, Or even -evasive- when it comes to money?.

Yet God Himself is very concerned about this 'real and pressing' issue?.

For God didn't create man to be needy or poor.

"And "God" is a Rich God"!.

Both in goods and in substance also!.

AND:

In -ideas- as well.

And that is an area we very often overlook.

Since God has rules and laws that affect wealth and prosperity?.

And yes riches too!.

Yes its -really-quite simple:

At the same time we "must" keep in mind:

That if we obey these laws!.

And work hard!.

We will know and enjoy prosperity,.

But the coin also has another side as well.

Being that if we disobey these laws and ignore Gods rules?.

Then the end result is always disaster, ruin and poverty!.

And wishing to avoid this state of affairs;

This book is designed to help you both to grow and also to prosper in your finances.

Which is really simple but:

"The catch 22 is that you **DO** have to obey the rules".

That then being the case lets take a clear look at some of Gods Rules & **Wealth Tips** for your economic success and prosperity!.

1. You reap what you sow!.
2. And you save what you reap!.
Or if you work hard, Save your money and invest wisely.

Then you will know prosperity.

But the Bible also warns that!.

"If you are lazy and stay home and sleep
then you 'will' know poverty,need and want"

In part then what God is -really- trying to
tell you:

1st RULE:

1.Quit feeling sorry for yourself!.
2.Quit making 'excuses' and follow God!.
3.Quit being lazy and get out and earn!.

Believe me -you'll- be glad you did,.

2nd RULE:

'Seed time and Harvest time"!.

Just like being on the farm and trying to
raise a crop?.

You -do- have to plant some seeds first!.

Now to study the matter a bit further:

'The seed for your "cash crop" can come
from many sources".

But if you don't first sow, Then you -cant-
reap the harvest.

22

And it is if you -keep- in mind that if you don't 'plant' your seed (cash) into good soil (Bank CDs, High Yield Bonds,Pension and Retirement Funds ETC!).

Then you cannot and "will not" reap a harvest!,.

Or put bluntly!.

You will not get paid!.

Remember:

That without seed time there is no harvest time?.

Yes God does reward hard work!.

But the 'choice' of what you do.

"Remains Yours".

3rd RULE:

"Never ever borrow money!.

This almost never works out!.

Granted on -some-occasions this has been of benefit?.

Yet many fail badly!.

Indeed many people remain poor all of their lives simply because they "build" their lives around borrowed money.

(Others peoples money)!.

Expressed simply borrowing money is one of the easiest 'bad' ways to stay chronically poor, starving and broke!.

"And permanently in debt?".

In fact one of the "main" reasons for the current "hyperinflation"!.

And the terrible financial crisis America is in that instead of creating real wealth!.

Is largely brought on by our 'poor' habit of borrowing money!.

(Both in the public and private sectors!).

And the Bible speaks so strongly about debt

Or against carrying a 'debt load' or a debt burden around with you.

After all we are told:

"The Borrower is the slave of the Lender".

Oh to be sure there are "emergency" situations?.

And sometimes people will borrow for good reasons?.

(A college loan, Or home loan etc!).

And yes at times to get some "working" capital to re-invest!.

The motives -may-be good?.

But borrowing money should be "shunned" and done only in an emergency.

True there may be some short term benefit.

But the risks are also real!,.

And the outcome difficult to be certain?.

And speaking of borrowing!.

All said above should be taken to apply triple to "credit cards"!!!!!.

And it can honestly be said that the bogus 'credit card- binge of "fake" prosperity!.

Strongly set the stage for the mass inflation and bankruptcy of the 80s!.

"Driving many to Poverty and Ruin"!.

True some see no harm in borrowing to reinvest?.

But given the "current" and shaky markets even this matter is doubtful?.

Now Jesus taught an 'important lesson' in the parable of the talent!.

Which we will examine here:

"This began with 3 Servants".

Now each servant was given something of value.

And as it turns out;

One servant lost his money!.

While another servant being fearful of loss buried his and hid it!.

Then the last servant being interested in 'profit' invested his money at interest!.

So that when his "master" returned the servant was able to repay the master with interest!,.

Now this definitely was an important lesson.

See "God" always desires gain!.

(As you should:Dear Reader!).

And even interest!.

Plus Jesus also tends to support this plan of action!.

And while this shouldn't be taken to justify every 'wild scheme' that comes your way?.

If reasonable means may be taken to 'secure' gains!.

And having ones "own means" of income is perfectly justified.

'And the Bible says so'!.

In fact if looked at carefully the Bible speaks of the Patriarchs having their own fields!.

And their own flocks!.

This alone makes it -perfectly- clear that God didn't just design;

OR:

Solely intend man simply to be a common day laborer all his life!.

To continue this line of thought:

The Bible also speaks of the desirability of having your own fields,.

And you own flocks as well!.

Both to see you less dependent on others!.

Plus to 'encourage' you to earn gainfully!.

And theres still more?.

Another good Bible principal is not to plant mixed seed when you grow a good crop?.

"True this can mean several things".

1.Find just one "profitable" area or item and stick to it putting your seed money in there!

2.Always invest or use the same amount when you do invest!.

(Don't mix your funding).

3.Learn to plant your financial seed in 'good' ground that is sure to give a generous return on your investment!.

As we should always remember that the Scripture teaches us to be fruitful.

And doubly so in regards to our finances.

As we should also seek gain when we can.

And profit in all that we do.

Not just for our own benefit!.

But always for "Gods" glory!.

For God is a mighty God!.

And whats more:

God is a God of Might,Power and Miracles!.

"Yes thats right".

God is a God of Miracles!.

And whats more He is also a God of Wealth.

Thats true!.

God is a God of Wealth!.

Now the Bible says:

That God gives the "power" to get wealth.

And wisdom and knowledge as well!.

See the Bible says this:

And there can be "no doubt"!.

After all we should remember that the word of God is true!.

"And also that the Scripture cannot be broken"!,.

Now then lets study these facts a moment?.

Yes plain fact and not "Hopes or Dreams"!.

But facts, Just plain and simple fact,.

Now we know that:

1. The word of God is true!.
2. And that the truth will set you free!.
3. And that the "Word" created all things

Yes we are to stand on the "Word of God"!.

Now we are starting to get somewhere.

For instead of hopes or dreams we are to 'use' the truth:

We are permitted to use the 'Word of God'.

And as the 'Children of God' we are heirs and "joint heirs" of the promise!.

"Exactly just like Jesus".

For we are 'joint heirs' of Gods mighty power!.

Keeping in mind that:

He (God) who made the promise:

"A -real- promise!.

And who "originally" spoke the word!.

(And -all- things into being!).

Has the power both to redeem (and keep) the promise that HE spoke into being!.

For He (God) is the great and mighty one who made the promise in the beginning.

Yes, Yes and by now I know Dear Reader!.

That many are shaking their heads and saying:

Fine! but this is really all just words, And this is all just talk:

"But how"!.

Or how then is this exactly all to get done?.

Yes thats right!.

(An excellent point indeed!).

Or lets just say:

How do I get my mortgage paid?.

And 'how' do I push the merger,Or the business deal through?.

And of course:

How do I buy a car to get to work?.

Or :

Oh if I could only get a bag of groceries?.

Alright these are the questions?.

And here is the answer!.

And here is exactly 'how' its done!.

"We have to speak the word with authority"

Just like we said at the beginning that God has certain rules (and laws) that apply!.

But that aside!.

We are to -speak- the word with authority.

And -with-power!.

And whats more we -are- to claim authority in Jesus name.

For we are to "command" the mortgage or home loan!.

(Or money,Or cash blessing to come!).

We are to -command- the merger,or business deal to happen!.

And speaking in Jesus name we are to command:

That the car (or if need be the auto loan) to happen!.

"To come forth"!.

And let there be -no- doubt about it.

It -will- happen,.

Sure it sounds amazing right?.

But not really.

Its not at all amazing!.

Not when you remember that God is a God of miracles, signs and wonders.

And God made the "promise".

(Confirmed by 'Jesus' own words).

And actions!.

That we should stand both on the promise and upon the "Word of God".

Thats right:

"The Word of God"!.

Thats sure.

And whats more you d be surprised to know all the -good people- who are "amazed" at this teaching!.

"One man told me":

"Sure I know we can speak or rebuke sickness and tell it to leave, But money"?.

Another said:

I -read- the Scripture but "didn't" know we could use it that way?

"SURE YOU CAN"!.

Just by standing on the word and on "Gods Power"!.

Because "God is Good"!.

And He 'loves us and wants to Help.

For "God is the God" who longs for prayer!.

So with thanksgiving and a 'joyful heart' I urge you to "pray for these things".

And any other good blessing that your heart desires.

As God cares!.

However I must -add- two provisos (Or conditions) to this?.

Not "my conditions"!.

But things that Jesus the Lord advised us Himself about!.

For in prayer Jesus said:

"If you ask in my name,I will do it!".

And again Jesus also advises that:

"You -Must- Not Doubt"!.

But these teachings aside;

Ask with joy and a loving God (for He is loving) may possibly even 'grant' your request,.

And in closing permit me to add that:

Always remember to praise and thank God!

(With Christ and the Holy Spirit also!).

For praise is a very great power in itself.

And is definitely pleasing to God!.

Helping to keep the blessings flowing.

So by all means ask that 'your' joy be made full.

For God is a God of miracles,signs and wonders!,.

Well: Dear Readers!.

Lets sum up then and see what we've learned from this Chapter?.

1.For lack of knowledge my people are destroyed!.

2.Poverty in the richest country on Earth!.

3.A person who saves money makes money

4.There is a difference between making money and saving money!.

5.The Bible advises us on 'financial issues'!.

6.People from all groups spend more than they make!.

7.Never 'ever' borrow money!.

8.That goes double for credit cards!.

9.The Debtor is the 'slave' to the Lender!.

10.Never spend where there is no return!.

11.God didn't create man to be poor!.

12.God has rules that affect wealth!.

13.Remember seedtime and harvestime!.

14.Remember the 'profitable servant'!.

15.Dont rely only on a job to make a living!.

16.The Scripture teaches us to be fruitful!.

17.Don't be dependent,Get out and earn!.

18.Jesus said:"Don't Doubt!".

19Jesus said Ask in my name and I will do it

20.God is a God of miracles,signs,wonders!.

And last but not "least" always remember to keep praying.

That is "Important"!.

"And -Keep- On Praying"!.

As not praying can easily lead to 'disaster'?.

Remember:

A man can have a 'million dollars' and still be broke.

"And why does that happen?.

Because "spiritual poverty" can and will lead to 'financial poverty'!.

It is -almost- certain!.

That being the case always remember to pray and give thanks to God!.

That is a "must"!.

Now that we've learned the lessons in full!.

But those "desiring" more information are strongly advised to read my earlier book on:

"Power Christianity"

It has a "LOT" of answers!.

BUT;

Its time to look ahead.

Let us move on then to the next chapter!,.

CHAPTER .2

FINANCE IN GENERAL

WISDOM WORDS

WITHOUT FAITH THERE IS NO VISION

Let us now look at:

Finance in General!.

Now let us keep in mind and carefully 'consider':

That there are many,many basic financial plans as there are separate investors?.

(And-almost- as many variations as well!).

"Plus there are many different investment advisors".

And 'quite naturally'!.

That being fully understandable as all our needs, priorities and goals are different.

And sometimes "very" much so?.

"Lets look at the differences then"!.

1. YOUNG PEOPLE!.

Of course young people (a few smart ones!) are investing now!.

Both to save retirement funds!.

And to build for the future!.

Now except for 'occasional" spurts!.

Young people tend to invest for the long term?.

Though 'house buying' may also be considered as a growth activity!.

Plus as a 'kind' of tax shelter at times!.

All in all a "wise" activity!.

Lets now talk about:

2. MIDDLE AGED PEOPLE!.

This then is an interesting group:

Now 'middle aged' people are pretty much "splitting" their investments?.

Splitting investments?.

Yes though they are still -value- investors!.

They prefer blue chip stocks, annuities, and high yield bonds!.

Basically they are riding the line between saving for:

1.Retirement Income.
2.Risky volatile stocks.

See expressed plainly:

They want "both" worlds.

OR:

They want security for the future!.

And "high" cash income now!,.

That can be a little risky and many people who speculate get caught in market crashes

(IE: Speculators are those who "gamble" with the Markets!).

Now middle aged people tend to do well but are still caught between the anvil of ;

Income now!.

Retirement later!.

(IE Investing in 'Risky" markets require timing,value. and lots of caution!).

Keeping in mind that Middle Aged investors are probably a large group (If not THE largest group) of investors,.

3. SENIORS /MATURE PEOPLE!.

We tend to sometimes overlook this group?.

And Older People do have a -hard-job trying both to budget their funds?.

Plus trying in addition to 'wedge' their savings and retirement benefits to live a bit more comfortably!.

"As they tend to prefer security together with high cash dividends".

Opposing 'risky' speculation and -unproven-stocks?,.

And God bless them as contrary to roumer or popular opinion.

Theres nothing 'wrong' or ungodly about financial prosperity or economic success!.

Of course the Seniors sometimes have special needs,.

Re financing secondary / retirement homes.

Helping at times finance education for grandkids.

And they at times have 'special' medical and housing/quality of life issues?.

So its clear that the financial need of this group will only grow.

And at a fast pace.

And most 'likely' so.

4. SPECIAL NEEDS INDIVIDUALS!.

Of course in retrospect we should glance at this final group of people!.

These people are different from most other wage/salary earners?.

This group can comprise:

Military/Government retirees.

Airline/Railroad retiree's.

Doctors/Lawyers/Small Business owners!.

This group mainly is composed of somewhat older "High Net Worth" individuals!.

And if you want to ad as a separate subgroup?.

Wealthy Widows/Lottery Winners and people who received inheritances.
Plus pension fund holders etc,etc!,.

Now this group tends to already have sizable cash assets.

So they tend to be more interested in both value investing,blue chip/high dividend and bond funds etc!.

They may already have along with cash sizable real estate and real property holdings in addition?.

(Expensive automobiles, Art,Antique items).

Finally this group also tends to be quite interested in tax shelters, And various other legal ways to minimalize income?.

But for all groups we -must- firmly keep in mind the need to:

1.Maximize income!.

2.Minimize risk and loss!,.

All of the above pretty much spells out the needs of all the "major groups" of a modern urban industrialized society,.

But again it must also be -stressed- that all these groups have one common denominator?.

Or a factor that overrides all groups!.

A "need" to earn or reinvest existing capital.

That being stated the questions remains is how!.

OR:

How do we invest!,.

Or more importantly?.

How do we reinvest as that is where the "greatest" bulk of the -true-profits exist!.

Frankly there are "many" ways to look at this problem?.

Now we know for a fact that "GOD" gives us the power to get wealth.

(That is certain!).

"Along with wisdom and knowledge as well".

Yet even with knowledge.

And lots of it!.

Why then is it that so many of these investment plans?.

Stock schemes,And pension plans have failed.

"Or are failing"!.

Indeed a -good-question?.

Looked at in the bright and stark light of day.

Put frankly there are many reasons for economic distress and financial failure.

Now in "recent" history!.

It would appear to fall into 3 categories:

1.The investment plans are not 'Gods Plan'.

2.The stock and bond funds and Investment clubs are not -well- thought out?.

3.The 'Human' failings of the financial planners and managers!.
(IE; Larceny and Greed!).

4.And of course 'unrealistic expectations" together with "simple miscalculation"!.

Have led to ruin, disaster and chaos!.

Both in financial markets.

And on an "unprecedented scale" nationally.

Granted Dear Reader some of the above sounds a -bit-critical.

And the possibility -does- exist that some of the recent economic 'collapse' was caused by 'simple' ill planning?.

Its stunning!

And all factors should be examined?,.

After all there is such as thing as dumb luck!.

"Right"?.

However if we take a hard look at the greatest teacher of all time.

Didn't Jesus Himself advise us about those who would despoil a house?.

"Or rob and steal"!.

True we can blame all the day long.

'However we have to face facts!.

The facts being that recent financial planning seems both to be:

1.Unworkable and Unsound.

2.A total and -inept-failure?.

3.Or just a -wild-scheme to defraud you out of your hard earned money!.

"Oh! The times that we live in"!,.

Not very long ago a financial manager stated quite frankly that:

"We don't have a market, We have a casino".

And another manager remarked that:

'Rapid trading is the key to the market because it increases profits despite ups and downs"?.

(Yes for the individual managers and brokers who charge for trades)!.

While interestingly enough Jesus also criticized the market of 'His time'?.

For not only did Jesus drive the moneylenders out with a whip!.

He also explained to the Disciples that:

"The day will come that all these stones are thrown down".

(Sadly and on a 'smaller scale' a part of that prophesy is now happening in our own time)!.

And Jesus was right to be critical of the financial policies of His time helping lead to war and the collapse of His country!.

And it sounds -shockingly- similar to our own time doesn't it?.

But there is Hope!

For we always have a 'firm friend' to stand with in Jesus,.

So lets keep in mind that your own 'personal' financial world doesn't have to collapse!.

OR:

If if it has (and the worst) is already happened,.

And you Are: "broke and ruined"?.

It -doesn't- have to 'stay' that way!.

For there are principals that can help!.

"Thats right".

"Bible Principals!".

So you can at least start digging your self or (herself) out from under the ruin?.

And rebuild 'more' firmly a sound and better future for you and your family!,.

(And hopefully with less pain also!).

Now Then:

In an 'earlier chapter' we discussed savings.

And granted that can be a controversial topic for many?.

But in fact:

It can be a "hard or an easy" topic!.

So most people I discuss the matter with tell me they just -cant- save.

All right I can accept that, But only on the surface?.

For in counseling sessions I've heard people tell me 'poker faced'!.

I cant save for a down payment!.

I -cant- save for retirement?.

Or the money "just" isn't there,.

Its very interesting to notice these people and their personal circumstances.

How one lady is dressed in very trendy clothes, But cannot save a dime?.

(Not at all what'd you'd buy at K-mart).

Or another man who discussed 'his plight' ,But who walked out to the parking lot climbed into a new car and drove away?.

And in another case one man assured me he had a desperate 'financial problem!.

That he never had any money!.

Yet he could be seen every afternoon right after work stopping off at a local 'liquor store'?.

Plus 'many other' instances aside!.

Perhaps the matter being that we have to exercise some discipline (or control) over our spending?.

The -hard- truth being that life is at times a trade off.

("Surely at times some very hard ones").

Yes 'sometimes' we have difficult choices about the things we need?.

And at other times about the things we really -don't- need!.

So it has to said and bluntly that:

"The 'real' key to financial security is savings".

Yes truly it is not easy to save.

Its hard!.

But its easier to follow: **WEALTH TIPS**!.

1. We become 'disciplined' buyers and sellers?.
2. We develop a program or goals to follow?.

For even the Bible makes it clear that there are no "free lunches" in life.

And God will 'surely' help you!.

But the -decision- in turn "really" rests with you!.

We should always remember that :

'Sometimes we have to make sacrifices today'!.

'In order to move forward tomorrow?,'.

And we learn that:

"Where there is a will, Then a way also can be found"!.

And you 'will' be surprised at the extra sources of cash that can appear if you look?

Perhaps -extra- income can come from a bit of over time, Or possibly a yard sale.

Other times we need to put off buying that new car, or even the new house for a year or two,.

Both to become stronger!.

And to put our selfs in a better position financially!,.

And we should always remember one -critical- fact!.

We -own- possessions!.

They -don't- own us!.

Oh! it is nice to have things but we should remember to keep things in perspective.

Our "first" loyalty is to God!.

After that all the rest comes into order!.

Like using our "savings" to put the -rest- of our 'financial house' in order?.

And we should seriously look at the savings plans that exist at work.

For sometimes your bank or credit union can also make withdrawls into a savings plan for you!.

And possibly:

At times perhaps a second or a 'part time' job may be in order?.

Both to help build up some savings and also some 'investment capital',.

Yes we -should- keep in mind that all earlier generations had to make some sacrifices!.

And of course accept a "few" trade offs in life to be successful,.

And sometimes we have to ask ourself s:

"What do we -really- want out of life".

Now a good way to plan all this out is to write it down on paper!.

(That is important!).

Then tally up what you want to achieve?.

A new car!.

A retirement fund!.

Or to send your kids to college or trade school!.

And then on a second sheet of paper write down all the trade offs to reach these goals.

To make it happen.

Then finally on a third sheet of paper write down all your purchases.

Especially all the "junk items" that you buy?

IE: Soda Pop,Candy Bars,Liquor or Tobacco!

Sure and you'll be surprised how much you spend on junk in a week, Or month!.

"Or a year"!,.

Maybe even enough to fund a 'nice' retirement for yourself?.

Now if -all- else fails a sure solution is?.

Just to get down on your knees and pray!.

Thats right just pray and keep on praying.

Tell God in prayer what is troubling you?.

And ask God to help you for God always has an answer!.

For God will find a solution, Or guide you in the right direction,.

This being said and done!.

Lets look ahead knowing that now we have set up a good savings program.

Plus we can 'expand' some of that into investments!.

And possible even start a small college fund for the kids.

Or even start funding a small 401k based retirement plan for yourself?.

See its easy when you think things out.

Now there are two ways you can go?.

1. One is to talk to the investment manager at your bank!.
2. Or you can arrange at your workplace or bank for a payroll deduction for either savings bonds or bank CDs?.

Now some prefer a more active approach and use an on line bank or brokerage!.

Do keep in mind with the current 'drastic' ups and downs of the markets.

That all investments must be entered and watched with some care.

If uncertain possibly your banker or investment professional can steer you between the rocks and the hard places?.

But to look at the 'very' basics!.

Its tends -mostly-to fall into three categories.

1.Long term investing for steady gains and retirement income!.

2.Mixed income with possibly lower earnings but more secure investments!.

3.Annuities and Bond Funds for cash income for reinvesting or retirement living!.

Those 'tend' to be the basics!.

But there are, And can be many -variations- of the above?.

Oh true some people and brokers swear by commodities!.

Others prefer to invest in gold or precious metals!.

And sometimes these things work out!.

The other side of the matter being that:

Many people are perfectly 'happy' with just their pension or retirement fund.

With possibly some good old U.S. Savings bonds to tide them thru the rough spots and to provide some security!.

Now some want to supervise their own investments?.

While others feel more comfortable with a managed bond or "Mutual Fund"!.

And true sometime you can balance the short but 'high risk' investments together with a steady but long term low interest bond?.

(Preferably a coupon or 'insured bond'!).

Still if you feel uncertain about what is right for your personal situation?.

Then perhaps a good talk with your licensed broker or banking representative can show you a 'clearer' way to invest safely!.

In this "rapidly" changing economy there is a definite need for caution?.

But in all cases please think before you act.

However in concerning finance and the Bible I can advise that:

1.The Debtor is the Slave to the Lender!
2.Never-ever- borrow money!.
3.Never -invest- money unless a return is guaranteed !.

This aside:

"Praise God in all things!.

And go 'forwards' in faith!.

Knowing surely that after Seedtime comes.

"Harvestime will -surely- be yours"!.

Now then lets review to see **WEALTH TIPS** we've learned from this Chapter!.

1.Be a disciplined buyer,Use money wisely!
2.Avoid investments without a return!
3.To save discipline/sacrifice are needed!
4.Write your expenses/goals out on paper!
5.The key to financial security is savings!
6.God gives us the power to get wealth!
7.Its important to-think-before you act!
8.Remember the decision rests with you!
9.In doubt remember to seek wise advise!
10.Praise God "always"!.

CHAPTER .3

CASE HISTORIES OF FACT

WISDOM WORDS

A PENNY SAVED IS A PENNY EARNED

So then to prove our point!.

We will reveal several 'case histories' of people who became quite wealthy.

"Using Bible Principals"!.

And perhaps one person who didn't?.

Yes granted that in a country like America practically anyone with reasonable intelligence?

Who also possesses common sense!.

And will work hard can in the course of time become quite wealthy given 'normal' circumstances.

Naturally of course there are always a fair number of "unbelievers" as well!,.

But at this point in time we will discuss these fairly plain persons who rose to some prominence!.

So to begin lets discuss key points about:

Sebastian Kresge!.

Although not 'well' remembered today Kresge was in his time a teacher,a salesman

Not to mention a very sharp business man.

And a generous Philanthropist also!.

Now He began his business by buying into several of the then new 5 and 10cent stores

Plus being both intuitive and a 'perceptive' man, When he saw opportunity he reached for it?.

For Kresge is the man who started the giant K mart chain which grew into one of Americas largest retail chain stores!.

It appears that in the beginning Kresge taught school for some years before becoming a salesman?.

And in fact Kresge was so good at this that he foresaw the rise of chain store marketing

So in 1897 he decided to do something about it.

Despite the fact that a 'business depression' was currently raging at that time.

Kresge took his limited capital and bought into a couple of early "five and dime" stores

Now that took guts and Kresge had plenty!.

His background:

Was modest and he came from a plain family.

Yet Kresge watched his cash and lived quite simply!.

Preferring to wear cheap suits and spending carefully and then only when he had to.

In other words he was "thrifty"!.

Still Kresge had vision.

And he was loyal in his 'Tithe and Offering'.

(Its said -extremely- so!).

In fact very probably -more- so than many others both before and after him!,.

"And God rewarded him richly"!.

For Kresge often did without necessities to pay God first!.

Knowing the teaching to put God first in all that you do.

And in -return- God will put you first in all that He does!.

So Kresge's business expanded rapidly and he incorporated his stores in 1912.

And by 1922 – 23 He had already amassed over 200 million dollars in wealth!,.

For Sebastian Kresge didn't forget God after he became wealthy?.

He then established a foundation and over the years put some 60 million dollars of his own money into it.

And whats more Kresge swore off 'Alcohol and Tobacco' preferring instead to concentrate on business!.

For just as importantly He took interest in his employees.

"And established both insurance and retirement plans years before other employers even considered them?".

Yet even though he was 'aging' Kresge would still personally visit areas to build new stores.

'And his God given talent for finding good locations was just as good in the 1960s as it had been back in the 1890s'!.

For the one unfinished goal of Sebastian Kresge was to live to see 100yrs!.

Well He didn't make it?,.

But God did allow him to see 99 years!.

And whats more Kresge lived long enough to see his plans unfold for a new type of store?.

A shopping center where all the goods could be located in a central place or location.

These "New Stores" would be called K-Marts in honor of Sebastian Kresge.

For Sebastian Kresge had a vision!.

Yet he remained true both to God and to himself,.

And there is 'no' better type of businessman than He who puts God first!.

So it has to be said that Kresge had:

1.Faith!
2.Vision!
3.A willingness to work hard!
4.Was good to his fellow man!
5.Faithful in his 'Tithe and Offering' !.

"He truly had all the ingredients of success".

And He did very well indeed!.

Now lets move on to the next individual.

So in our next "profile" we are going to look at another amazing man?.

A man who helped change both his time!.

Plus the world we live in today?.

That being the case it can be fairly said that

Henry Ford was an amazing man!

And Ford is well remembered for many things that changed modern history,.

He started life as a common farm boy.

Then became a tinkerer!.

A mechanic,And in time an engineer also,.

And after all this He also started the :

"Ford Motor Company"!.

Now outwardly Henry Ford was not openly religious?.

But he did attend Church at times!.

And the foundation he established together with his charitable gifts.

Helped his fellow man considerably!.

Ford was a plain man in his lifestyle.

Still he had energy, And was also a man with considerable vision!.

He was a very controversial man at times?.

But He lived and worked in hard times together with a changing world.

Henry Ford could be kind at times,.

On occasion He would personally stop and help people repair their broken cars by the roadside.

Other times He could and did run his factory like a slavedriver.

And was known to be 'strict' in his business affairs?.

To be fair to Ford it should be said that:

He tread the 'middle ground' between kindness and hardness and it was a 'delicate' balance!,.

For Henry Ford fought the unions and organized labor to a standstill!.

Yet He was one of the first employers to hire blacks and other minorities in number!.

As Ford remembered His days on the farm and the hard work that blacks did in the fields.

And Henry Ford wanted men who would work the same way in his factories and shops.

Plus He paid a very generous wage!.

In fact one of the best salaries in Detroit which allowed working people to actually buy some of the cars they produced?.

Ford struggled during the depressed 30s both to keep his factory open and the workers employed!.

Still after a fight that turned -nasty- in one of His factories Henry Ford called labor management in?.

And offered the unions better terms than any other employer in the auto industry!.

Even though He was aging Henry Ford realized that he would have to adapt to the changing times he lived in?.

So its clear except that for an occasional stubborn streak Henry Ford was no different than the rest of us,.

He wasn't a saint!.

But he wasn't an evil man either!.

No! not by any extreme?.

Like 'most men' who lived in -difficult- times he tried to steer a middle coarse !.

(And so should the rest of us!).

Yet given His background and beginnings:

Henry Ford had amazing insight both on how to solve a problem?.

And on how to "simplify" something and to make it less complicated.

In designing His most famous car 'The Model T' Ford !.

Ford was careful to keep the parts simple.

Yet making it easy to repair if a part broke!.

And The Model T designed to be built on an assembly line making it inexpensive enough so working people could easily afford it!.

For it was produced in enough numbers that in 1920 half the cars in the whole world were Model T Fords!.

And Henry Ford didn't stop there?.

In the 'middle' of one of the greatest economic depressions in History!.

Ford was not only able to provide funding enough to expand his Factory.

But was also clever enough to buy out all his stock and shareholders as well!.

So that Henry Ford became the complete and -sole- owner of "Ford Motor Company".

Leaving him 'effectively' in absolute charge of the company.

And even a stroke hardly slowed the now elderly man down at all.

In fact Henry Ford had to resume operating control of the company during World War II.

Its clear that all considered Ford was truly a blessed man indeed.

He did have some 'struggles' in life!.

But he lived well into His 80s.

And before passing on Ford shook his head in wonder at some of the new trends in the auto industry?.

He started out a farmboy but finished a 'millionaire'.

It doesn't get any better then that!.

See then what a person can accomplish if they combine:

Vision, Hard Work and Bible Principals!

And theres -still- more!.

Lets then examine another case shall we?.

Personally I myself think that John D. Rockefeller was an interesting man.

He worked hard, had vision and imagination:

"And whats more he used them".

Now Rockefeller was a strict teetotaler!.

Who professed Baptist beliefs all of his life!.

In addition to being 'Loyal and Faithful" in Tithe and Offering as well!.

He lived plainly and strictly and monitored his spending carefully.

Plus he had a good education coupled with strong powers of organization.

Which he made ample use of:

Of course it was to his good fortune that John D happened to live in the time before income tax?.

And 'government' -over-regulation- of business enterprise!.

Still in the very beginning Rockefeller came from a poor home.

But with drive and energy he 'overcame' his poverty stricken background.

Becoming a clerk John D worked hard and continued to study.

"Being determined to advance himself"!.

And after taking a long hard look John -did- have some good fortune in establishing himself in both a new and also a growth industry?.

"Oil".

Granted that during this very first part of Rockefeller's career the automobile was unknown,.

But there was a serious and necessary need for oil which was then used in lighting!.

For by John Ds time America had advanced away from candles?.

Which had been the mainstay of lighting since colonial times.

In turn relying on the 'oil lamp' as electric lighting had yet to be invented.

Now by the time of the Civil War whale oil,paraffin and other oily substances had become way too expensive to be used!.

But it had been found that kerosene could be made rather simply from crude oil?.

And John D seized the moment forming his own oil company,.

Basically Rockefeller's oil company or "Standard Oil" as it became known!.

Was simply a shell for a group of small companies that John D and his partners had pieced together during the 1860s and 70s.

And Rockefeller organized his firm with an eye both to expansion, Preferring himself to concentrate on profit making!,.

For as America expanded westward John D made sure that Standard Oil expanded with them.

As Rockefeller used both common sense and financial acumen to build his business.

Now at first the oil business was 'loosing' money?,.

The problem being in the wooden casks or kegs that were used to ship oil at that time.

As they were simply wooden kegs held together with metal hoops and bands.

Still they were both expensive and time consuming to make?.

So Rockefeller hired a clever tinkerer to work on a new cask that was easier to build and also used less metal in its construction.

And as it turned out the new drums could be made faster as well and at a cost savings

Being so successful that in its first year alone the new drums saved over 1 million dollars!.

And put Standard Oil into the black!,.

In recalling the matter John D liked to say:

"My first million I didn't make, I saved"!.

Well John D. Rockefeller faced many more challenges as the 20th Century began?.

And times had changed!.

People changed and the world also had changed around him?.

But John D didn't change!.

He kept right on Tithing and Offering,.

And He -shunned- Alcohol and Tobacco.

And God blessed him and John Ds business expanded until he was:

"Americas First Billionaire"!.

For He saw the fruits of his labors living on until 1937!.

Still John D. Rockefeller lived to see a world radically different than the one he had been born into.

And one he had helped bring into being!.

Building a fantastic future for himself as well,.

So Rockefeller was an amazing man.

And we can easily see the power of Faith, Tithe and Offering.

Carefully noting how important they are?.

They truly are!,.

That then being the case let us go on then and look at one last case study:

"A Lady"!.

Yes a very interesting lady named:

"Henrietta -Hetty- Green"!.

She was a 'nondescript' person and somewhat plain in appearance,.

Being born abound 1843 in an old and established Maine family.

So established in fact that some of her ancestors had even came over on the "Mayflower"?,.

In -fact- Hetty was no plain personality.

Her situation was very unique!.

After all Hetty was a women.

And that gave her problems being accepted as a 'business person' in 19th Century America?.

As the business world was largely 'male' dominated at that time.

Yet Hetty wasn't 'dirt' poor either!.

In fact both her father and grandfather had become wealthy by operating their own fleet of whaling ships,.

And in truth when Hetty's father died she inherited a fortune estimated at between 7 to 10 million dollars!.

Sadly Hetty Green has been much maligned both in the media (especially the press) in her own time.

(IE: Mainly the late 19th and early 20th Centuries).

And today in our own time as well.

The real truth about 'Hetty Green' is probably 'somewhere' in the middle,.

While still a child Hetty had apparently learned the Quaker virtues of :

Hard Work, Thrift and Charity!.

And Hetty Green expressed Quaker beliefs all her life!.

But somewhere and tragically things didn't work out for Hetty?.

Because despite her sound beliefs it must be added that Hetty could be:

Mean, Spiteful and Vengeful at times!.

"And Cheap"!.

Yet even that is -open- to interpretation as one persons thrift is another persons savings?,.

Still even with 'some' sympathy for Hetty its hard to read contemporary accounts of her life and not come away with the feeling that

Something had somehow gone "badly" wrong!.

Her Father had died suddenly and some felt he may have been poisoned?.

And Hetty also had a marriage that failed.

(Yet she had 2 children?).

But Hetty may have crossed the thin line between "Honesty and Dishonesty"?.

And spent several years living in England to avoid being 'prosecuted' for fraud!.

However in time she returned to America and set up headquarters in New York City.

Hetty then it appears set up an office of sorts in the Chemical Bank Building,.

She then became quickly one of the shrewdest stock traders in New York!.

Though being somewhat 'dissatisfied' Hetty later switched directions getting involved in the securities business?.

And also in issuing "high interest" loans to businessmen,.

Apparently Hetty's experiences in England affected her deeply!

For when she did return to America it appears that Hetty preferred to stay on the move?.

Living in a series of cheap hotels and rooming houses.

Partially to dodge tax authorities and other investigators she feared were dogging her footsteps?.

Now 'Hetty Green' was a paradox!.

She often was angry, mean and cheap?.

Yet she could be generous at times in her donations to churches, charities and to poor and destitute individuals.

But she pinched pennies to dire extremes!.

And Hetty refused to buy herself a 'decent meal', Instead preferring to eat cold and ofttimes -rancid- porridge?.

But she'd spend countless thousands in court suits trying both to prosecute (and persecute) her enemies!.

This 'despite' the fact that she had been raised as a strict and charitable Quaker.

And amazingly enough Hetty had herself re-baptized in the Episcopal Church in old age;

So she could be buried in hallowed ground next to her deceased husband?.

Granted that Hetty had Christian beliefs.

But many people wondered if Hetty was simply a complicated (if somewhat vindictive) person?.

Or perhaps a slightly 'unbalanced' lady who had crossed the line between sharp business practice?.

And violating the strict Bible warning against "worshiping" mammon or money itself as a god!,.

Still we need to look at Hetty's activities with some charity given the many ups and downs in her life?.

Truly its hard to say?.

But Hetty Green or the 'Witch of Wall Street' as many had called her had been fortunate in many ways.

She lived both to see the 20th Century!'

And also lived to the ripe old age of 82 finally passing away from a stroke in 1916.

After a 'violent' argument with a cook no less!.

Now Hetty lived long enough to see the 10 million her parents left her multiply into 100 million dollars.

And she has been listed as one of the 40th richest people in history

Indeed Hetty Green was probably the single richest women in the United States in 1910.

However given the misery in her own life and the suffering she caused in the lives of those around her?.

Its very doubtful if Hetty Green really enjoyed her wealth!.

But her estate was huge indeed.

So together with her extensive real estate holdings.

Hetty Greens total net worth may have exceeded 200 million dollars at the time of her death?,.

A-rather-large sum!.

We'll Dear Reader:

Its up to you?.

Who would you decide to be?;

Sebastian Kresge with his thrifty goodness!

Henry Ford with his boundless energy!

John D. Rockefeller the King of Oil!

Or Hetty Green the 40th richest women!

True all of these individuals had faith!.

(At least to -some-degree!).

Though it has to be remembered that they were born and raised in the 19th Century.

And 19th Century America was a 'vastly' different place than it is today?.

To be sure.

Plus one of the individuals!

Hetty Green started out with 'inherited' wealth.

But also had to struggle against 'gender prejudice'.

Also they did for the most part have vastly different goals?.

Yet they did share the following.

1.Religious faith!
2.A willingness to work hard!
3.Vision in what they were doing!
4.Exhibited some degree of leadership!

And they all applied **"Bible Principals"** and became wealthy!.

Plus they also all "believed" in God!.

And all had 'Faith" and very much so!

So Dear Reader the decision is yours?,.

Now then lets look ahead to the next Chapter:

"The Nuts and Bolts of Financing"!.

There are **"Wealth Secrets"** there!,.

CHAPTER .4

THE NUTS AND BOLTS OF FINANCE

WISDOM WORDS

NEVER WASTE TIME FOR IT IS LIFE

Now in an earlier chapter we 'discussed';

"Basics of Finance"!.

However this is a book written in General?.

Or rather:

A book written for everyone,.

And that -includes- those to whom finance is a mystery?.

So Dear Reader:

Here we give you the nuts and bolts of finance!,.

"With a few **"Tips and Tricks"** tossed in for good measure".

So looking at the matter,For nothing is certain in anything.

And -that-includes 'finance'?.

We'll try and keep this simple!.

(And non technical!).

You have two basic choices to make money?

You can use the following **WEALTH TIPS**:

A. Save and Invest!.

OR:

B. Work and Earn!.

Now theres a lot to be said 'for both'?.

Or depending on how "hard" your willing to work!.

Or how much time and -determination- your willing to devote.

Some people can use parts of -both- to raise them to the pinnacle of "financial" success!,.

As always the 'bottom line' is always you!.

Now given that times are -very- uncertain right now?.

Some prefer the 'lower' but more secure investment of U.S. Savings bonds?.

Whereas others may prefer a good mutual or bond fund where the managers run the fund for you!.

But you reap the profits!,.

Some who are willing to accept more risk?.

Prefer to "speculate" during the day!.

Say some on options?.

While others like the ups and downs of currencies?.

Yet some would rather use a 'computer' and dabble in the Asian markets at night!.

(Its daylight over there at that time!).

Personally Id avoid the riskier stuff as timing is critical.

And either you have it!.

Or you don't?.

Its well to keep in mind especially if your funds are very limited, Or you are risk averse?.

"Like me"!.

That a war torn depression riddled economy entails -risk- so be very sure what you put your money into!.

For now mutual funds and insurance annuities 'seem' fairly safe!.

But it "doesn't" hurt either to do a little detective work at times!.

After all the Bible says to "make sure"?.

(A good thing to keep in mind?).

1.a How sound is 'the company'?.

b. In the last 3yrs have their earnings gone mostly up (Or mostly down)?.

c. Have the main managers or CEOs been fired or retired in the last 3yrs?.

d. How are the stocks for volatility?.
(Steadily rising,Or dropping like a rock?)

e. Does the company have high liquidity?.
(Do they have cash or are they 'broke').

f. Is the stock couponed?.
(IE: insured against loss!).

g.Check out the legal briefs and court news!
(Is the company in any kind of legal/tax trouble?).

h. Are any of the top or leading corporate officers being investigated or under indictments of any kind?

"A Google search here can 'reveal' a lot"!,.

And its always good to look at the 'upfront'
or side money you earn from investments.

Does the stock pay a good or better yet;

A nice 'strong' dividend?.

And are the dividends paid regularly?.

Or have the payments ever been reduced!.

Or even suspended?.

Granted that if a Company is good and
strong that a stock split is desirable!.

(Unless it causes loss of value?)

But splits must also be watched carefully as
it may show "instability" (or weakness) in a
company.

See its important to watch problems as
anything major can make a stock lose value

"Which means you lose- BIG -money".

And also driving down other markets as well

So its clear that to profit in todays markets
it takes:

"Knowledge and Wisdom"!.

And to gain major profit now it also takes:

1. Caution!
2. Timing!
3. Clear thought and planning!
4. Strict discipline and spending control!
5. Firm 'goals' that must be followed!
6. Lock your -profits- in or clear out!.

 So its easily seen from all of the above that investments today in the 'current' markets are -very- risky?,.

Especially so with violent swings and 'wild' gyrations in markets that make gambles in paper and securities an "open" question!,.

Yes in more 'normal' times concentrating on "High Yield" markets was the way to go!.

But in todays markets such an approach can lead to disaster due to "sudden and disastrous" market drops?,.

(Even in -normal- times also!).

That being the case:

It appears that a more balanced approach would bring better results.

And it should be remembered that these are 'uncertain times?.

In addition that instability in securities tends to spill over into bond markets also sooner or later!,.

Possibly a more cautious approach might be to play "the spread"?.

Say if pharmaceuticals, plastics and manufacturing are up!..

Doesn't it make better sense to buy into a little of each rather than buy heavily into one .

And taking a "drastic" loss when it collapse?

After all isn't steady gain better than sudden and total loss!.

(As just happened to many quite recently!).

Or for retirement isn't it better to have some investments in a good growth company that has a coupon bond paying a "high" dividend?.

Then "risky speculations"?,.

Oh to be sure I am aware of the famous 'stock guru' who advised against buying a stock just because it had a good dividend.

Unfortunately this man also came to a tragic end!.

And -killed- himself when his own high risk portfolio collapsed!,.

"Yes dividends can be controversial".

Myself as I explained the point to one man:

If a company is too poor,Or so desperate that it cant afford to pay me a decent dividend on its stocks?.

Then why should I "risk" investing in it!.

(It just doesn't -make- sense?).

Now personally I think that balance with a little caution tossed in is just fine!.

(Especially in 'risky' times!).

So perhaps in looking at the matter you decided to put say;

30% in a mutual fund and possibly 30% in a good high yield stock with a dividend?.

Now the last 30% could be divided up say:

10% in bank CDs!.

10% in a money market bond account!.

10% say in antiques or gold coins etc!.

That alone would still leave you with 10% left over.

Which could be kept liquid in cash for emergencies or other needs?.

So its clear that many interesting scenarios exist?.

And many exciting possibilities remain open to chance!.

However the decisions 'remains' yours,.

See we need -always- to keep the Bible in mind!.

Both in our 'lives', And also in our investing!

In fact some of the best advise ever given is located in **"Psalms and Proverbs"**!.

Granted there are many many rules that will help your money grow!;

Or your business to grow and expand,.

Say as a rule of thumb if a business or financial plan can grow at a rate of 30% a year?.

"Then that business will almost "double" in about 3 years time".

Also keep in mind the **WEALTH TIP** that:

One of the 'oldest ' and best laws in business is the Law of Supply and Demand!.

Or 'put simply' if you -really- want to prosper and get rich?.

(And who doesn't!).

Then find something that people really want?.

"And need"!.

Buy it up at a 'cheap' or closeout price.

And go and resell it at a big mark up!.

(In fact Dear Reader thats how I expanded my Internet business),.

And you'll be surprised at the money you can make.

Another item people often overlook is the power of compound interest.

"In fact Lord Rothschild once called it the 8th wonder of the world".

Say if you were able to just take 100 dollars and double it, And keep on doubling it in the coarse of a year;

Then if you never touched the interest but just let it keep multiplying.

The case being over the coarse of about 20 years it would build up to around 50 million dollars or so!.

(A nice 'bit' of change!).

After all the big secret (Or **WEALTH TIP**) is in the multiplication.

And an -even- bigger secret is not to even "touch" the money period!.

Now if you take the interest and re-invest it and "keep" re-investing.

And just keep reinvesting it.

Then just see where you are at in a year or two.

"Or three".

For the old saying is true that:

'It all Adds up'!.

Lets keep in mind that there are:

Laws of Supply and Demand!.

Laws of Increase!.

Laws of Use and Multiplication!.

Laws Not to Borrow!.

(IE: Not going into Debt!).

Or to express it plainly;

"GOD"

Or if you prefer the "God of the Bible"!.

Has 'Rules and Laws and Ordinances'.

That is indeed a fact!,.

And History shows and teaches us simply that if we obey God!.

That we will prosper, succeed and are blessed.

Now the other side of the coin is also true?.

Being that if we 'ignore' or -disobey- God!.

And reject His teaching and rules?.

We end up being defeated and undone.

And in "extreme" cases destroyed!.

So its clear that to become wealthy?.

We need to work, plan and reinvest!,.

For its clear that both technology and the world itself is both changing and evolving.

For even 10 short years ago who would ever have thought that the home personal computer?.

(In the 1990s largely an expensive toy!).

Would have become a mainstream tool both in business and in finance itself!.

Ands whats -more- a very useful tool both for worldwide communications.

Plus tracking investments as well.

As with the right 'software' and a high speed net connection.

Its really quite easy to manage your own savings and investments online.

Or through an established online bank or brokerage firm?,.

So looked at from 'all' sides its truly amazing what can be accomplished with good discipline.

And a "clear" goal in mind!.

And the amazing things that can be done with a small and relatively cheap home computer?,.

Lest we 'forget' we should keep -firmly- in mind that nothing is free in life.

Or in investing?.

However in the next chapter we will explain some rules that God has made to help you!.

And to -make- you quite rich as well,.

That being the case: Dear Reader.

Lets do a 'quick' review to see what we've learned from this chapter?.

1.Never ever waste time!
2.Have a firm goal and a sure plan in mind!
3.Secure investments are good!
4.Always invest in sound companies!
5.Only buy insured bonds with a high yield!
6.The best securities are 'managed' !
7.Never ever spend your profits!
8.Watch for violent drops in the market!
9.Remember to spread your money around!
10.Money doubles at 30% a year!
11.Never go 'willingly' into debt!
12.Use a computer to track your spending!
13.Always consult a licensed professional when in doubt!.

And finally lets "remember" to always praise God daily!!!!!.

For we know -surely- that God is the "real key" to all things.

"And that includes wealth"!.

So then to close this out:

Lets move ahead to the 'next' chapter and see what God advises in our finances.

Never doubting and "always" believing!.

For God promised to bless us;

Keeping 'firmly' in mind that He who made the promise.

"Surely has the power both to keep".

And to -redeem- the promise!.

That "He Himself" has made!,.

"And bless Him for doing so".

AMEN!.

CHAPTER .5

GODS PLAN FOR WEALTH

WISDOM WORDS

TO RECEIVE WE GIVE

Now "God" has at times not 'revealed' certain matters to us!.

(No doubt for reasons of His own?).

And Jesus himself has 'taught' us through parables!.

"But God has been very plain in teaching",.

'Even Blunt'.

("And He needed to be").

At times concerning our lives, our personal affairs;

Our 'relations' to Him!.

In matters of 'Divine' worship to "Him".

And at times concerning our money and financial matters.

And well He should have!.

For money is a important (tho complicated) matter?.

'Truly much -careful- reading'!.

(And a -**LOT**- of study!).

Of all related matters.

Of technology!.

But "best" of all.

For Psalms and Proverbs is needful to anyone who is both serious and careful as to his (or her) her finances!,.

"And -that- is certain".

However in earlier chapters we've reviewed certain critical teachings from Psalms and Proverbs in regards to finances?,.

IE: The Debtor is the Slave to the Lender!.

And Lend but do not Borrow!.

Plus:

A person 'should' be established!.

And:

'Have your own field or flock.

Or 'means' of livelihood!.

Or in plain English:

To have your own 'means' of earning a living!

Instead of just depending on a job?.

(IE: Job means Just- Over- Broke!).

As many 'well meaning' people are finding out today.

Oh to be sure there is nothing wrong basically with -working- for an employer!.

Or indeed with working hard at all.

"Provided of coarse that":

1.You are strict/committed in your savings!
2.You are firm in your investment program!
3.You have a good pension/retirement plan!
4.You also have an emergency fund!.

To cover emergencies,sickness layoffs etc!,.

And last but not least?.

Possibly you also work 'part time'.

Or better yet?.

You have your own business or means to earn cash.

"Plus I -very- strongly advise you to re-read all of the above".

To Help you!.

And also to help put your own house in order.

(And that includes your financial house)!.

Now its becoming -very- clear that our prosperity and our financial well being are 'very' important to God!.

'Indeed its super clear'.

Even Crystal:

As God through the Prophets advised us in Psalms and Proverbs!.

And yes many people are completely unawares that;

God Himself!.

Yes Dear Reader.

That God Himself in His wisdom has set-up His -own- financial plan for us.

Yes thats "completely" right.

God Himself has set up a 'financial plan' for all of us!.

Thats right "Dear Readers"!.

For all of us:

'And that includes You and Me'!,.

And its all for us.

For -are- we not the Children of God?.

And are we not the handiwork of Gods great pleasure.

So that shows us how much that God Cares.

After all God has to regulate 'everything' on earth!.

Starting with the Sun and the Moon and even beyond the Stars.

And ending with the tiniest Bug and all the hairs on your very head?.

That 'My Friends' must be a real -workday- for any one!.

Still God cares so -much- for you.

And for me that He takes time off from His own daily tasks to help us set up our "own" personal financial plan!,.

And its a 'good' plan!.

And God must have taken a lot of time to work this out,And like everything He builds!

It is both flawless!.

And indeed it is picture perfect.

So what is the name of:

'Gods Financial Plan'!.

It is called 'Tithe and Offering".

Thats right just: **Tithe and Offering!.**

And it is such a -perfect- plan that no insurance company or bond fund could ever have worked it out.

'Much less than even thought of it?'.

Now God is really concerned about your financial prosperity.

"And your future".

So He has worked out the planning for 'Tithe and Offering' to your benefit.

Yes its -true- you don't have 'to join' the financial plan?.

And even tho God -feels- strongly about the plan.

'God being always a Gentleman He will not make you join it',.

Thats the type of 'God' He is.

"For God is a -caring- God!".

And in truth most people do not "belong" to the Plan?.

"Thats right they don't belong".

For that truly is -very- profound?.

"And even amazing".

Granted it is -incredible- that most people don't belong to the "best" financial plan there is!.

And it is even Tax Free as most religious offerings are considered 'tax deductible'!.

(Just ask your tax advisor?).

Yet Dear Reader Id like you to consider one 'vital and essential point'!.

Considering that most people -refuse- to participate?.

Thats right -they- refuse to participate.

"And thats their right".

'Now then:

Most people -do- not belong!.

And yet if you look carefully Dear Reader:

"Thats right look carefully".

And take a 'good' look at your friends and neighbors as well.

Now here comes the "main" point!.

OK so most people do -NOT- belong to Gods financial plan.

They refuse to obey Gods rules (and laws) for financial prosperity.

And just 'look' at the result.

As most people are "needy and poor"!.

And many others are being laid off or otherwise are loosing jobs and homes also!.

Some are even starving and desperate.

"See its starting to make sense isn't it"?.

People refuse to obey Gods rules!

People -refuse- to join Gods financial plan!

People refuse to take part in Tithe/Offering!

So its hard to escape the obvious isn't it?.

That People are becoming jobless and homeless at an 'unprecedented' rate.

"Its amazing and astounding"!.

And yes its 'horrifying' to even consider that:

Poverty and Want -exist- in the 'Richest Country' in the world!.

And what even worse?.

That Hunger,Homelessness and Need are happening in the "Land of Liberty"!.

Its sad to be sure but the facts are there?.

More and more people who are just plain folks like you and me!.

"Everyday people like you and me are going 'flat broke" in broad daylight?.

And loosing everything they own in the bargain!.

(Including -whole- families as well!).

Now Id like to add here some brief commentaries from several social workers!.

Now during the last Depression some people conducted surveys among the huge masses of homeless and jobless persons.

Really just everyday people who were poor and destitute and in doing so?

One man explained that:

"Having asked many individuals who had lost both homes and jobs I find that;

'Nobody who'd been loyal in their "tithe and offering" was jobless or begging for a hand out'!.

Now another social worker remarked.

Having talked to several ex-millionaires they were both amazed and appalled in their findings?.

"I asked one individual if during the time of his wealth he had been -loyal- in his tithe and offering".

This man looked at me blankly and answered:

"No I wasn't and I've -lost- everything".

And this same question was asked of others and their reply was "staggering"!.

And the men couldn't answer?.

"They just looked at the ground and shook their heads shamefully"?,.

So it can be seen that it is a 'very good' thing to be loyal in:

"Your Tithe and Offering"!.

As 'God' feels "very strongly"on this issue!.

For He is -deeply- concerned in any area that seriously affects mankind.

So concerned in fact that God Himself once stated:

"Will a man rob God?,But you have robbed me in tithe and offerings"?.
(MAL 3:8).

Also:

"For you rob me even this whole nation".
(MAL 3:9).

So it is 'clear' that:

You will be 'blessed' in regard to your loyalty in paying your "Tithe and Offering".

Now tithing can be paid in -many- ways?.

Now the usual way is to pay 10% of your earnings!.

But in some instances for 'very poor' people a tithe can be the tithe you give to help the Lord.

One man couldn't afford to pay tithe, But he helped clean a local church for free after services!.

So perhaps the time you use in 'witnessing' or in passing out leaflets?.

Or even helping a neighbor to the store may be considered an offering.

"God is -not- unreasonable".

But he does expect His fair share!.

Now offering is 'different' than tithe?,.

See the tithe is the money (or service) you return to God as Thanks for his kindness to you!.

The tithe actually belongs to God and is His by right,.

(After all 'He" has more than earned it).

Now then the Offering:

So basically the offering is -your-money?.

It is actually your money 'free and clear' after the tithe that you pay to God!.

Now there "are" countless types of offerings

And reasons for giving?.

(Yes many, Many reasons for giving!),.

Examples being:

'Say sometimes you need a favor for a friend ,Or a loved one?.'

And sometimes when God answers prayer it is 'polite' at time to give Him an offering.

(That is just being proper).

And possibly you have a 'little' left over from the bills?.

Or your -investments- prospered so you give God a extra offering!.

"True God really doesn't need our change"!.

(He is "MORE" than powerful enough to get the job done!),.

But it "really" does help His work.

And whats more it does -show- you care!.

For believe me God loves what you give.

For the Lords work is dear to His eyes.

(And those who help in that work!).

So if you are really serious about
prospering in all you do?.

Or even becoming wealthy!.

"Then just start paying your tithe and
offering and you will prosper greatly".

For the 'Tithe and Offering' is like any other
financial plan.

To get Cash out you have to put Cash in
period!.

OR:

To gain a Harvest there must be a Seedtime
first?.

And then you will get a 'Harvesttime' later!.

And "believe" me that:

Money and or service rendered to the Lord
is always the -best- investment you will
ever make!.

The Bible even says so.

There is -definitely- no doubt,.

And 'God' agrees for He states:

"I will rebuke the devourer for your sake".

And in showing how you will prosper God also says:

"I will open the windows of heaven and pour out a blessing"!.

Yes and it doesn't get any better than that,.

Just read the book of Malachi its all in there.

So now lets sum up and see what we've learned from this Chapter.

And gather the Details from "Our Study"!.

1.Poverty and Hunger in the Richest Nation!
2.God has a financial plan!
3.To get Cash out, You have to put Cash in!
4.Gods financial plan is: Tithe and Offering!
5.For Harvest time there is Seed time !
6.Not paying Tithe is "robbing" God!
7.God regulates -everything-on Earth!
8.Wealth depends on your Tithe & Offering!
9.The decision rests "on you"!
10.God cares!.

Thats right Dear Reader!.

Theres no 'getting around it?.

"Tithe and Offering" are important!.

Yes its true that some have became wealthy and haven't payed Tithe and Offering?.

Yes thats very true to be sure.

But again:

How many have gained wealth.

Or have become famous?.

And have gotten a good job or a career.

Only to lose everything?.

Plus seeing all their hard work vanish completely and forever!.

"Simply because they -didn't- follow Gods rules".

Or "refused" to follow Gods financial plan for success?.

Yes its sad and 'tragic',But its true!.

You My Friends must judge for your selfs,.

And -granted -its really hard at times,.

To be sure?.

And to know and to decide?.

And when to fold.

And when to act!.

And -that- time is now!.

And sometimes the best "**WEALTH TIP**" is to just get out and 'act now'!.

And while this is a 'Bible' based guide!.

I think it may prove useful to some to include in the next Chapter:

A short article on the History of Investing.

And I am sure you will find it informative!.

Lets move ahead to the next Chapter then!

I am sure you will enjoy it!,.

CHAPTER .6

A BRIEF HISTORY OF INVESTING

WISDOM WORDS

NOTHING VENTURED
NOTHING GAINED

I think that both to clear the air a bit.

And also to help fix our focus a 'little' more on finance.

We should examine in a few brief pages a short:

"History of Investing"!.

Granted that finance and investing go very far back into both the early history and 'possibly' even the prehistory of mankind?.

Yet it is very clear that basic economics.

And mans -desire-both to invest and to gain wealth reach back almost to the earliest reaches of antiquity!,.

So it would seem that temples and places of religious worship functioned as the worlds "first banks".

'And possibly at times as a type of exchange or clearing house as well'.

For they were secure!.

And also being -constantly- watched.

Together with a type of moral or social stigma?;

125

That existed against robbing or stealing from temples and houses of worship that tended to put off even hardened thieves?.

Now then for many centuries this type of arrangement tended to work very well!.

However:

Later on it seems another type of commercial activity appeared that became known as "Buying and Selling"!.

('See the 'Bible' principal of buying and selling was established even at an early period').

But as we were saying about Buying and Selling?.

Or if you'd rather restate the matter as:

"Trade and Commerce"!.

It appears that both 'Trade and Commerce' tended to -begin- mainly at the behest.;

(And in the hands of).

Private traders and or "wealthy" individuals'

And very quickly became highly specialized.

This being so.

Then this possibly?.

Was the very first or early appearance of what we would now call banking.

True in the earliest or rather more formulation stages the term 'Bank' didn't -really- apply to a building.

Or a 'fixed' place of business?,.

But rather to an individual, Or a group of wealthy individuals who "together" made up a lending institution.

"Or a Bank"!.

So together then this bank or group of 'wealthy individuals' helped to make financing and resources available.

To help in the expanse of Trade and Commerce.

Al tho in Britain and later on Europe the term:

'Financial or Banking House';

Was to linger or hang on for a very long time?,.

Still we have to look at the other side of the coin!.

After all what did a person do.

Or what if someone wanted to start a business!.

Or simply just needed a loan to tide them over?.

Then where did "these" people go.

Needless to say it would seem that lending.

Or obtaining a loan also appeared from an early date?.

(Possibly a very remote period of time?).

It would seem that people could borrow grain and then promise to repay the debt with interest at a later date.

So maybe grain/food was the first currency?

From that it seems that an early type of credit or commodities trading was born?.

From ancient records we know that grain and tools were both traded and held for security or collateral on loans,.

And this was so even in -early- Babylonia!.

So business and trading grew hand in hand,.

Yet the possibility remains that perhaps the practice originated in 'Ancient Egypt"!.

(But the exact origin is vague and unclear?)

So its quite plain that the 'Bible Principals' of lending.

And also to "Establish Yourself".

Plus that of "Buying and Selling"!.

Were not only established.

But indeed were well entrenched and practiced from a very early time!.

Now as to the beginnings of coinage or money?.

Now this is an important matter!.

And indeed it does get interesting here?.

Now paper money apparently originated in China.

(And -why- not for wasn't paper invented there!).

So it appears that at first paper money was used mostly as a type of promissory note or loan perhaps?,.

But at a 'later date' paper currency was also issued to help cover both Gold and Silver shortages as well.

(Interestingly enough this was also one of the reasons Paper Money is introduced into the U.S. To cover Gold shortages during the American 'Civil War'!).

And the very "great" advantages of paper money were quickly realized?.

It was a -lot- lighter than coins!.

Plus large amounts were relatively easy to carry in the bargain.

Not to mention that it preserved scarce Gold and Silver for other uses also?.

And naturally it didn't hurt investors (Or speculators!) at all using paper money.

Or its "little brother" the promissory note!.

Still its interesting to 'note' that the first speculators were Babylonian grain traders,.

Let us move "forwards" a bit?.

Now by the time that the Renaissance arrived in Europe both banking and trading had advanced to the point;

Whereas ship cargo's were used as security.

And even speculated in!.

So naturally money could be lent out at variable rates (according to risks involved!).

And 'currency trading also began to appear about this time.

(As rates on gold and paper varied widely).

Now it was the Italians who brought "Modern Banking" to Europe!.

This was relatively easy as Italy being basically a peninsula surrounded by water.

Had ready access to the sea and served as a gate way to the rest of Europe.

And Venice served as a conduit both for currency flow.

And the early China trade that helped ferry tea and silk into Europe.

(Plus Arabian spices and perfumes!).

Still Banking had a 'hard start' at first and didn't catch on for a bit?.

Partially as the Italy of that time was very unstable!.

And that some of the Monasteries and the 'Religious Orders' also did a type of banking

So naturally they didn't like to be competed against?.

And the trade tended to benefit the large numbers of traveling businessmen and religious pilgrims visiting the Holy Sites!,.

So it seems that Modern Banking!.

(And 'Banking Houses')?.

And the growth of "Exchanges" began in a very basic way around various London Coffee Houses.

Now from these Banking Houses and Exchanges;

(Mainly small currency traders at first!).

Banks and Exchanges of 'varied types' spread rapidly.

Though in the beginning it was mainly the port cities.

(London, Liverpool and Bristol).

Where Banking was most needed at the time,.

Which of coarse was natural as ocean shipping which could carry both profitable cargo's and passengers would need financial services?.

(And Lending services etc!),.

Once the English practice of Banking appeared profitable.

(Actually -quite- profitable indeed!).

Then it spread from there quite rapidly across the Channel to Europe and the rest of the Continent!.

And of course in time the use of Banks spread from Europe to the rest of the English speaking world.

However in America the Banking system ran pretty much (at least at first) along English lines.

(Not greatly surprising as the America of that time started as a English colony?),.

Yet it would seem that the "Exchange Business" didn't really take off until after the Revolutionary War of 1776?.

In fact Alexander Hamilton who had been a General during the Revolution!.

Had advised starting a 'stock exchange' to help pay off the American war debt of some 10 million dollars!.

(An astronomical sum at that time!).

So with help from one of Washington's former Generals.

Together with help from New York bankers and businessmen?.

"The New York Stock Exchange was born".

Of course the rest is all pretty much history.

Naturally the exchange adapted itself as new means and technology of transferring communications opened up,.

And of course to try and curb some of the abuses then regulations had to be passed to help keep the markets running smoothly!.

(But that is outside the scope of this book).

Still it remains quite clear that investing has a long and distinguished history.

And it even helped channel the forward development of 'modern' times!.

And a -very- important history,.

But this simple and straight forward outline will help those unfamiliar with banking and investing.

Giving you some idea of how these things function and even came about in the first place?.

So that being the case!.

Lets do a "Quick Review" and see what we've learned from this Chapter.

1. Temples were probably the first banks!
2. Grain trading was the 1st investment!
3. Babylonians were the 1st investors!
4. Early banks were wealthy individuals!
5. Paper money originated in China!
6. Italians brought banking to Europe!
7. Exchanges began in London coffeehouses!
8. Early banks started in "Port Cities'!.
9. U.S. Exchanges started after 1776!
10. Exchanges use modern communications!

"Now that we've looked into the history of Finance".

Lets move ahead to the next Chapter.

For we can -always- learn from the Bible!.

And "Bible Men of Wealth" will be good to look at!,.

CHAPTER .7

BIBLE MEN OF WEALTH

WISDOM WORDS

AND THE LORD BLESSED THEM

However in an earlier Chapter we discussed case histories of certain famous and 'wealthy persons' who through Faith!.

(And theres -nothing- wrong with Faith!).

"Plus some vision"!.

And 'Lots and Lots' of hard work?.

Helped these people over the course of time to become "quite wealthy"!,.

Granted Dear Reader:

And many will say?.

That hard work together with sacrifice and 'savings' will make anyone wealthy over time.

True! but if you look at the record its also quite clear that "God" helping people tends to -provide- more wealth and prosperity.

"Than not"!,.

So there is 'Right and Wrong' in -both- view points.

Perhaps in all things maybe 'balance' is the answer?.

But just to prove a point!.

Let us take a closer look at some wealthier people and well go from there?.

So at the start we know that Adam the 'very first' man was placed in charge over the Garden of Eden!.

True Adam wasn't 'wealthy' in Silver or Gold as we would look on it today?.

"Yet to keep things in perspective".

We should remember that back at the dawn of history the -initial- concept of wealth hardly existed.

(That would come much later and during another time).

'But Adam was given an -important- job.

"And God trusted him to do it"!.

True "He" could hardly have given it to anyone else?.

Still it was an important position.

And God did -entrust- it to him.

(And God doesn't do that with just anyone).

Of course at first everything went well!.

But as it would later turn out?.

Adam like "many others" forgot what he was told.

"GODS WORD"

And -just- as bad if not worse!.

Adam took his eyes off God and wound up following some very -bad-advise?,.

In these pages its not important to go into exhausting detail about the fall of Adam.

(And Eve the very first women)?.

But we do 'know' from the Bible that:

1.That Adam and Eve were "kicked out" of the Garden of Eden!

2.Adam -was- fired!

3.And was the -first- man in history to both get Fired.

4.And also lose an 'Executive Position'!.

Granted that many others came after Adam and that some were successful!.

And some were not,.

While many others tried?.

"And -most- failed miserably"!,.

Now this "pattern" of repetitive success and of countless failure went on for very many centuries.

(And countless 'civilizations' rose and fell during this time as well).

Still if we start at the beginning?.

Or perhaps just a -bit- after it.

We meet a man called Abram.

Now after a while God renamed him 'Abraham'!.

Yet Abraham is fairly well known as one of the 'Patriarchs' in the Bible.

That being the case the many ups and downs in Abraham's career and family are well known!.

(Actually quite a lot of ups and downs?).

From what we -do- know Abraham may have been fairly prosperous when he lived in UR of the Chaldees?.

Yet for reasons of His own God liked Abraham!.

"He really liked him"!.

For God liked him enough to rename him!.

(From Abram to Abraham!).

See God definitely likes to "transform" people even before He makes use of them!.

But back to our story!.

Anyhow God called Abraham and told him to leave the city of Ur.

God explained telling Abraham that he would be given the land of Canaan!.

Now Abraham being a fairly successful trader in cattle (or so the saying go's).

So Abraham packed up and went off to Canaan like God had told him;

Now Abraham must have looked out over this burning and desolate region possibly scratched his head a bit wondering?.

"Leave Ur for this useless Desert"?.

Truly that would have been a challenge.

And a daunting challenge it was indeed.

But Abraham remained -loyal- to God!.

And as a 'businessman' with vision he may well have recognized the great-untapped-potential that Canaan represented?.

And surely Abraham had Faith!,.

Unfortunately space prevents us from exploring Abraham fully in these pages.

(Though you may wish to do so later in your Bible).

But we know 'definitely' that Abraham was blessed.

And he even visited Egypt for a time?.

And once He arrived in Egypt Abraham did have some dealings with Pharaoh!.

(Or the King of Egypt).

And these dealings were exceedingly profitable.

For we know that when Abraham left Egypt he had both herds and flocks.

"And yes even servants too".

So clearly God loved Abraham and "blessed" him throughly!,.

Yet Abraham was much more than just a 'common' nomad.

"Or a simple herdsman"!.

Even the Bible testifies to that;

For Abraham was a wealthy man.

And he was rich in:

Cattle, Silver and Gold too!.
(Gen 13:2)

So its both 'Easy and Clear' to see that belief in God profits a person.

(And very much so).

And not-just-Abraham?.

But many many others as well.

And some in "great difficulties" also!.

So in speaking of difficulties lets take a look at the next case shall we.

The story of Joseph is also interesting and one can learn much from it?.

Now this isn't Jesus earthly father.

But a -very- different individual.

This man is the famed Joseph whose mother made him a coat of many colors!.

That being the case.

It seems that this Joseph was sold into slavery by his older brothers.

A sad story to be sure as Josephs older brothers were jealous of him.

So selling him off to a passing slave trader seemed to be a way of getting rid of him?,.

(Just short of course of 'outrite' murder).

Joseph it appears was a type of prophet or seer!.

(As we would call him today).

As God for reasons of His own 'decided' to send him dreams?.

Yet God also gave Joseph enough wisdom to interpret or understand the -hidden- meaning of the dreams as well!.

Anyway 'tiring' of Joseph and his dreams?.

His older brothers sold him into slavery!.

Then concocted a story telling their father that Joseph had been"eaten"by wild beasts.

After that it appears that Joseph eventually wound up in Egypt?.

(Now it gets interesting)!.

At first Joseph was well liked in Egypt.

He had ability and he worked -hard- and in the course of time Joseph did well and also became fairly prosperous!,.

Which is not 'too' surprising considering that God clearly favored Joseph.

However in Egypt Joseph did encounter some very considerable misfortunes?.

And though 'no fault' of his own Joseph was tossed into prison!.

But "God" did -not- forget Joseph.

Either in Egypt!.

And certainly not 'in prison' ?,.

Oh to be sure Joseph was -**NOT**- happy in prison.

(And who would be).

But God did not abandon him either.

Foe even in "Prison" Joseph had kept his amazing gifts of 'Dreams and Prophesy'!.

And the King of Egypt a man called Pharaoh had heard both of Joseph and of his gift.

Now Pharaoh had a dream and it troubled him greatly!.

So explaining the dream to Joseph who listened carefully and who gave the answer?

That the dream had 'foretold' a long period of famine for Egypt.

And Pharaoh believed what Joseph told him.

In fact he believed this so -strongly- that to all intents and purposes Pharaoh appointed Joseph his right hand man,.

Or if you prefer 'overseer' over all Egypt!.

So when the famine came Egypt under the watchful eye of Pharaoh.

"And the firm hand of Joseph".

Was more than ready to face the challenge.

For the average people were so desperate that they sold everything they had!.

Just to buy food to feed themselves during the famine time.

And naturally Joseph being placed over all the house of Egypt!.
(Gen 41:41).

"Became -**fantastically**- wealthy"!.

That being the case its clear that the story of Joseph shows what happens when:

1.We believe in God!
2.We continue in faith never doubting!
3.We work hard to the best of our ability always trusting in God for the answer.

And as we can see that the answer always comes back to:

1.**God!**

AND :

2.**Faith!**

But to close our tale about Joseph!.

Not only did Joseph become both wealthy and esteemed.

But in the course of time Joseph was also reunited with his family?.

Which is -very- much the way God works as He likes to insure a happy ending!,.

Now then:

To close on Bible men of wealth!.

Let us take a quick look at King Solomon.

In todays world 'King Solomon' is mostly remembered for:

"Knowledge and Wisdom"!.

But in addition Solomon was -very- wealthy also.

Indeed and King Solomon was quite probably the richest man of his time!.

Basically King Solomon became ruler when his father King David died.

Now for the first part of his reign Solomon ruled wisely and well.

Unfortunately as he aged Solomon started drifting away from the Lord!.

And started running into trouble?.

(A fact you and I should also remember ,Dear Reader!).

But during the heyday of his reign Solomon had fantastic wealth!.

In fact according to the Bible He needed whole cities just to store it in,.

And whats more King Solomon even had his own fleet of ships as well?.

It appears that Solomon wasn't just a King.

"But also a **Business Tycoon** as well".

Truly Solomon as long as he stayed loyal to God had "Amazing wealth".

And not only did he have wealth as King but many people also gave him wealth.

Thats right!.

Just to hear his words of Wisdom people even 'gave' King Solomon wealth.

And the Bible itself even bears this out.

In one famous incident the "Queen of Sheeba gave Solomon wealth.

And one account says:

They gave Solomon 'Gold and Precious' stones!.
(1st Kings 10:10).

And its clear Solomon was given other things as well?.

The wealth of 'King Solomon' is -almost- unimaginable to modern man!.

Even the ancient chroniclers say this.

In Fact:

"In just one year King Solomon made "over" 600 talents of gold!!!!!.

A truly 'mind boggling' sum even today?.

And by carefully re-reading all the accounts its clear that:

1.God loved Abraham the Patriarch!
2.God helped Joseph!
3.God indeed blessed King Solomon!

So now lets do a 'quick review' to see what we've learned from this Chapter!,.

For the "Famous and Blessed" men of history cannot be ignored.

This being the case then lets see what we have learned?.

1.Abraham showed that faith is important!
2.That God 'keeps' His promises!
3.Joseph had the special gift of Prophesy!
4.And that God saves always!
5.King Solomon shows the blessings of God!
6.As long as we keep in step with God!.

So Dear Reader:

Who would you like to be?.

1.Abraham who God loved!

2.Joseph who God saved!

3.Or Solomon who God blessed!.

Truly a -HARD- choice it would be?,.

"Now Then":

In 'closing' this Chapter permit me to thank
you for your patience!.

And to 'urge' you to carefully re-read the
Chapter!.

(And your Bible).

So as to -learn- carefully from the lessons
therein.

Now let us move on to the next Chapter!,.

CHAPTER .8

CONCLUSIONS

WISDOM WORDS

**IS THE END THE BEGINNING
OR IS THE BEGINNING THE END**

In closing its easy to see despite our efforts to simplify the matter.

That 'Finance and Investing' is far from an easy topic?.

Plus many persons!.

And yes even with "Gods Help"!.

Have had trouble,And even serious setbacks on occasion?.

(Joseph in Egypt is a -good- example!).

Its plain that to sum up investing requires;

1.Discipline!
2.Strong planning and -lots- of vision!
3.A 'whole' lot of hard work!
4.And a "lot" more faith!.

It clearly breaks down into 3 essential principals.

1.High risk for high gain!
2.Moderate to low risk for low gain!
3.Variable investing for security!

In retrospect Dear Reader:

You "know" your own needs better than anybody else!.

So it is -your-responsibility to see what course of action is best for you.

And of course what level of "RISK" is acceptable for your investment?.

Personally -MY- risk level is low and I always advise 'caution'!.

But the best rule of thumb is:

Never ever invest more ,Or put up more cash than you -CAN- afford to lose

Now together with a 'good' savings program

And council from your banker and broker!.

You may with Gods blessing make out very well.

But in the last option please don't just simply take your last dollar in the world!.

And toss it away on some "wild scheme"!.

Thousands of good and innocent people are victimized this way every year.

And I've seen several cases myself and its a sad thing to see.

For we should always remember Jesus advise!.

About just casting your seed "cash" into the Rock (Just wasting it)!,.

Thats why I always council firm adherence both to **'Bible Principals'!.**

And consulting a professional before you actually invest hard dollars in -some- "iffy" deal?,.

As sadly in our world there are always those who will seek the 'unwary' to take unfair advantage.

For its always been true that a dollar firmly in hand is better than two or three just hoped (Or gambled for)!.

And speaking of those tempted to gamble!.

You' d be surprised to know that even when the game is honest?.

(And many aren't).

The odds tend to run in favor of the house say about 7 to 1.

And lottery tickets are on the par at about 11 million to 1 against you winning the jackpot?.

So if you are tempted to gamble only do so for pleasure!.

But never for profit!.

(The ODDS are heavily 'against' you!).

After all doesn't the Bible teach caution?.

And the teaching does say to!.

"Make Sure"!.

Keeping in mind that a good knowledge of Bible principals.

Along with wisdom in savings and in investing will take you far!.

Both in your life and in your circumstances.

However if nothing else please learn two things from this book?.

1.Always save your money when you can!

So you will be ready to meet the need!.

And the second thing to remember is:

2.Always love and praise God all your life!

As praising God not only helps but it can open many many doors in your life.

Including some you can never imagine?,.

In fact a 'Wise King" once said!.

Make God your partner in -all- that you do
and you will always prosper!.

And thats a "wise" choice.

With God on your side you 'cannot' fail.

But -without- God you are beaten before
you start.

So by all means praise God and good will
happen in your life!.

Keeping also in mind that if you have not
yet accepted 'the Lord' into your life then
this is a good time to start!.

And with Jesus on your side you cannot fail.

Always keep that fact firmly in mind.

Both when you pray.

And in your life.

So believe me when I say that:

1.Its never too late to pray!
2.Its never to late to ask Jesus to come into
your life!

That is Important!.

After all weather you have 5 dollars in your pocket?.

Or 5 million!,.

If you have God then you always have something that you can be proud of.

Now at the end Chapter Ive included some information that may be of help to you in your journey,.

Instead of just putting it in a separate book as many would do?.

(And making you pay for it!).

As a 'courtesy' to you dear reader I include it free gratis in this book!.

AUTHORS NOTE:

I make -NO- claims about any of the companies listed.

But simply Include them as a starting or point of reference.

All other decisions are left to you!,.

"Now Then"!.

Lets review and see what we've learned so far,.

1.Discipline is good!
2.Planning is 'very' good!
3.Never put your money into risky schemes!
4.Never spend more than you can afford!
5.Always -check- the risks first!
6.Buying and Selling can help you earn!
7.A dollar in hand is "always" good!
8.Never -invest- your very last dollar!
9.Always consult a licensed professional
10.Ask your BBB for information!
11.Always save money when you can!
12.Praise God and good will always happen!

Alright My Friends:

We are nearly at the end of story here?.

I hope you've enjoyed this book and the lessons enclosed here!.

Plus the tales and parables enclosed I am sure have entertained you.

After all it took some of the wisest men in history many centuries to record them,.

And now I dearly Pray that God may both "Guide and Bless" you in all that you do.

"And may you enjoy success and prosperity"

And My Best Wishes To You!,.

C. Edward Royce,.

CHAPTER .9

EPILOG

Wisdom Words

**HOME IS THE HUNTER HOME AT LAST
THE SAILOR IS HOME FROM THE SEA**

Well Dear Reader:

Congratulations we've finally reached the last Chapter in the book!.

And nearly reached 'journeys' end as well.

So its time now for a last few 'closing remarks'?,.

True if you take a really hard look at investing or finding the means;

Indeed or any means to grow or multiply your money.

Yes I know its both interesting.

And exciting also!.

"Yet We Must"!.

Never 'ever' should we loose track of the Bible meaning?.

1.Worshiping False Gods!
2.Or worshiping "mammon"!

(An -evil- false god/"fake god" of money!).

Or -even-worse?.

That we get 'so' concerned about the affairs of "this" world;

That we may well forget?.

(After all we are human).

Yes indeed my friends.

We run serious risk of -forgetting- the one;

"True God"!.

('Hallowed be His Name!'),.

So as can be "readily" seen, The horrible risk of becoming rich?.

But losing our 'souls' seem -hardly- worth it?.

"Yet sadly enough it has truly been that way in all ages!",.

And from all earlier civilizations of mans existence on Earth.

Oh to be sure there is "nothing" wrong with being wealthy in itself?.

It is ,And can be a 'Great Gift' from God!.

But it carries Heavy Responsibility with it?.

Though properly used is a wonderful thing!

Now as long as we learn to keep things in balance then it is alright.

For surely we never want to take our eyes off!.

"HIM"

Nor should we ever forget:

Or forsake the 'Great and Mighty" God of creation?,.

Who is our Father as well!.

But all of the above aside.

Use your money as you will.

After all you worked for it and earned it!.

And it is yours to keep.

And to use as you will,.

For surely many many persons in history have been Wealthy?.

But how many have fell short of the mark?.

Perhaps like all things Dear reader;

The answer lies with you?.

And the "question" remains?;

What do you really want out of life?.

To be like Sebastian Kresge who tithed heavily and who prospered greatly?.

Or is Henry Ford the farm boy turned Auto Tycoon more to your liking?.

And we 'very much' need to remember!.

Hetty Green who was a nice lady in the beginning.

But who later let her money run away with her?,.

And there is both 'Truth and Story' in all of the above my friends.

For money like -life- itself is the 'Gift of God'

And you are free to use it!.

Or to abuse it as you will?.

"The choice as always".

'Rests with you'!.

Best Wishes.

C. Edward Royce,.

CHAPTER .10

RESOURCES

I hope you enjoyed our little tour thru the ins and outs of Bible based Finance.

But before we close out this book I am adding as a courtesy to you dear reader.

Some additional sources on financing .

Now unlike other authors I enclose this material;

"Free Gratis"

Instead of putting it all in a separate book and "Making" you pay for it?.

AUTHORS DISCLAIMER:

I Must Ad at this point That I do **NOT** Personally -endorse- any of the companies.

So any contact you have with them.

Or any business or agreements therein you do with them are '**Solely**' on your -own- accord!,.

However I simply add these as a 'public service' for your personal use.

From free resources in the 'Public Domain!.

Personally I oppose loans.

But I recognize that given the nature of the times we live in;

And the special needs and possible emergencies that may arise at times.

I add the enclosed material for your own usage!.

So please use 'due diligence' in all your actions.

Note:

The following list is intended simply for 'reference' only!.

1. General Loan Resources!.

www.eloan.com
(PH: 1-888-533-5333)

www.lendingtree.com
(1-800-555-8733

www.americaoneunsecured.com
(1-800-457-6785)

www.prosper.com

2. Student Loan Resources!.

www.studentloan.com
(1-800-student)

www.chasestudentloan.com
(1-800-487-4404)

www.discoverstudentloan.com
(1-877-728-3030)

www.estudentloan.com

3. Home Loan Resources!.

www.ditech.com
(1-800-ditech-3)

www.getsmart.com
(1-800-438-7627)

www.quickenloans.com
(1-800-251-9080)

4. General Interest Sites!.

www.ceoexpress.com

www.clearstation.com

www.mihran.com

www.cnn.com

www.reuters.com

www.softpedia.com

www.37.com

Thats about it!,.

But for a last -Perk- I include a final tip on.

"WEALTH SECRETS"

10 Rules to Remember!

1.Control Your Spending!

2.Always Increase Your Earnings!

3.Save Wisely and Often!

4.Invest Only When Sure of Profit!

5.Never 'Spend' Your Earnings!

6.Multiply Your Income Streams!

7.Spend Money Only To Gain!

8.Lend But Never Borrow!

9.A Dollar Now is Better Than None!

10.Remember To Praise God Always!,.

The End!,.

www.ingramcontent.com/pod-product-compliance
Lightning Source LLC
Chambersburg PA
CBHW051517170526
45165CB00002B/508